PRAYERS
AT MEALTIME

Sister Mary Teresa, O.P.

Novitiate Library

PAULIST PRESS
New York   Paramus, N.J.   Toronto

Library of Congress
Catalog Card Number: 72-91457

ISBN 0-8091-1745-2

Published by Paulist Press
Editorial Office: 1865 Broadway N.Y., N.Y. 10023
Business Office: 400 Sette Drive, Paramus, N.J. 07652

Printed and bound in
the United States of America

CONTENTS

Dedicated to
The Sisters at Maria Regina
who welcomed creativity

INTRODUCTION

These short prayers are original, except for those as indicated.

I have used them at table in Maria Regina Convent, Uniondale, New York, during 1971. The Dominican Sisters liked them. I thought, therefore, that other People of God might appreciate and use the little creations.

The meals may be long like dinner or short like lunch, but the prayers are brief and thankful for an ever ancient gift—food. They may clarify the Hebrew proverb: "He who eats and drinks, but does not bless the Lord, is a thief."

Whatever good a Christian does should reflect the glory of God (1 Cor. 10:31). Christ showed the way. "Have you caught anything, friends?" our Lord asked the disciples on their last picnic as they fished by the Sea of Tiberias (Jn. 21:5). A good thing then happened; Jesus cooked breakfast. Such hospitality, friendship, and providence became the inspiration for successive Christian meals.

Through these table prayers we thus review many events in the life of the Lord. Like us in all things except sin, He took His meals every day. At weddings or on the outskirts of cities, in homes of poor as well as the rich I consider that He usually ate in common with others and said grace before and after His meals (Mt. 14:19). "By His presence Jesus confers on meals their full value" (Pierre-Marie Galopin). His meals occasioned togetherness, salvation, reunion, courtesy, solemnity, joy, and renewal. Happy the table to have Him as Guest!

But most of all, perhaps, is the fact that Mass itself is a sacrificial meal; the altar essentially a table; the offertory, the setting of the table; the preface, the table blessing; the communion, the eating by the community standing around—a family meal of God's children. The bread and wine represent a great deal of human labor, and as food they stand for human life itself. The Mass is a very social arrangement, even to table conversation (John Harold Miller, CSC).

I think it is very significant that the Lord Himself asks us to contemplate Him under the form of food—sacramental bread and wine.

Since the feast celebrated in heaven, where God is the Host, is presented in the Bible frequently under the image of a banquet, I have concluded the booklet with Scripture quotations. Happiness, contentment, merriment, brotherliness, and intimacy with God are suggested by the imagery.

Sister Mary Teresa, O.P.

PRAYERS BEFORE MEALS

1

O Lord, may our bodies be refreshed and our friendships strengthened by partaking of this meal together.   Amen.

2

We cannot live on food (or bread) alone; neither can we live on love alone. So give us both. O Lord.   Amen.

3

We are not so poor that we do not have enough to eat. But, dear Lord, we would be

poor if we forgot to include Your poor in asking
for Your blessing at this meal.   Amen.

4

O Lord, give us both kinds of bread:
of this table and of heaven.   Amen.

5

Let us praise God for His gifts and
break bread together in His name.   Amen.

6

The disciples at Emmaus knew Thee,
Lord, in the breaking of the bread.
May we also get to know You and all of
us as we eat our daily bread today.   Amen.

7

This food, O Lord, is for life and life is
for You.
May we offer them both to Your loving
care.   Amen.

8

O Lord, You have asked us "to feast on all the good things You have given us" (Dt. 26:11).

May we not forget the hungry and the strangers who live in our own native land. Amen.

9

O Thou who said: "I am the bread of life" be now our bread of joy and consolation in each other.   Amen.

10

Food and drink are Your gifts to us, O Father. May Your blessing and our prayer sanctify our very eating itself.   Amen.

11

O Lord, may the table of the Eucharist, of Scripture, and of this meal lead us to Yourself.   Amen.

12

Your graciousness, O Lord, supplies us with all we need. May we in turn use all our energies for You.   Amen.

13

It is written in Deuteronomy 8:10: "You will eat and have all you want and you will bless Yahweh your God in the rich land he has given you."
Let us fulfill this scripture in our lives today.   Amen.

14

May this meal in common be a sign of our union of mind and heart.   Amen.

15

Let us eat and drink peacefully of the (name foods) God has provided for us today. Amen.

May we serve You, O Lord, in the joy and happiness that come from an abundance of all things (Dt. 28:47). Amen.

17

This (breakfast or dinner) is our Nazareth now. Please share with us, O Lord, Your sentiments as You sat down each day to eat with Mary and Joseph. Amen.

18

May this meal, O Father, help to create us anew by refreshing our lives. Amen.

19

Dear Lord, You accomplished great things at meal times: Cana, the Last Supper, Emmaus.

Help us also to fulfill Your will at this table. Amen.

20

Our Father, who art our Provider, blessed be Your name for giving us our food.

Give us also the energy to work for it and thus fulfill Your heavenly plans. Amen.

21

As we eat, listen, and respond to each other at this dinner, Lord, may we also do the same gracious things to You. Amen.

22

Lord, You once prepared a morning meal of bread and fish by the Sea of Galilee. It is now our turn to say to You, "Come and have breakfast" with Your 20th century disciples. Amen.

23

Here we are, O Father, at our family meal.

Please make us share someday a yet more glorious banquet in heaven.   Amen.

24

May we take this meal with gladness of heart, O Lord, rejoicing that we belong to You and to each other.   Amen.

25

We eat bread together at this (morning, evening) meal, O Lord. Its many grains suggest our union among us and with others. Some had to plant and harvest the grains; others had to knead and cook it.

Bread represents us here, dear Lord. We offer it to Thee.   Amen.

26

At Thy Eucharist, Lord, you nourish us body and soul.

At this table, may we be fed bodily and be a comfort to each other by our presence and conversation.   Amen.

May these (vegetables, meat, salad, etc.) bless the Lord as do the stars, moon, and the sky.

For these are your creatures, O Lord, meant for the service of man. We praise You for them.   Amen.

Give us, Lord, a bit o' sun
A bit o' work and a bit
          o' fun;
Give us all in the struggle
          and sputter
Our daily bread, and bit
          o' butter;
Give us health, our keep
          to make
An' a bit to spare for
          others' sake.
Amen.

          (part of an English prayer)

May this meal prepare us for the supper of eternal life.   Amen.

30

Give us a good digestion, Lord,
And also something to digest;
Give us a healthy body, Lord,
With sense to keep it at its best.

(English prayer)

31

Bless, O Lord, this food to our use, and us to Thy service, and make us ever mindful of the needs of others, in Jesus' name.   Amen.
(Traditional Protestant)

32

Bless us, O Lord, and these Thy gifts, which we are about to receive from Thy bounty. Through Christ our Lord.   Amen.
(Traditional Catholic)

33

Lift up your hands toward the sanctuary and bless the Lord. Blessed art Thou, O

Lord our God, King of the universe, who bringest forth bread from the earth.   Amen.

(Traditional Jewish)

34

Almighty and everlasting Father of us all, we thank Thee for this repast, which strengthens and nourishes our bodies as Thy eternal Spirit sustains our souls, and enables us to do good for others in Thy name and in the name of Thy Son our Savior Jesus Christ. Amen.

(Traditional Orthodox)

35

Bread is living when it is Yourself, dear Lord. May this other kind of bread on our table strengthen us in its own way to live for You and for each other.   Amen.

36

Come, Lord of the harvest, and rejoice us with Your gifts spread on our dining room tables.   Amen.

37

O Lord, who spent most of Your time on earth at home in Nazareth, be present to our (morning, noon, evening) meal in our house today.   Amen.

38

May we who eat here in union and brotherly communion also taste intimate union with You, O Lord.   Amen.

39

Here we are two (and or more) at table, Lord. Make Your glory felt as we eat our meal together.   Amen.

40

We cannot afford big banquets, Lord, but we can praise You for our daily meal. Amen.

41

Renew us, dear Lord, day by day in mind and body as we take our meal at our table(s).   Amen.

42

Let there be peace and contentment at our table, Lord. Be our joy.   Amen.

43

May we find Your love, Lord, in this happening of our eating the (morning, evening) meal together.   Amen.

44

We're hungry, Lord. Come and have (breakfast, dinner) with us now.   Amen.

45

Say but the word, Lord, and both our food and our friendships will be wholesome. Amen.

46

We come together to take our daily and ordinary bread, dear Lord, and to celebrate our life (lives) with each other.   Amen.

47

Let us seek Thee, Lord, and Thy kingdom so that we may not want in the good things You continually provide.   Amen.

48

The earth is the Lord's! Let us rejoice in what He has afforded us at this table! Amen.

49

May this food we eat become our living bodily cells, O Lord, and share in the life of the Trinity within each of us.   Amen.

50

As much as we need this food before us, Lord, let our souls ever hunger after Thee. Amen.

51

Fill us at this morning breakfast with Your kindness, Lord, that we may shout for joy throughout this day.   Amen.

52

We all look to You, O Father, to give us food in due time, as at this table.   Amen.

53

We eat our humble crusts of bread with peace, Lord. Keep strife from us at this table. Amen.

54

Bless the food and drink of your servants here, O Lord. Please provide for the wants of others and keep us safe and well.   Amen.

55

Even our food, Lord, can be made holy by the grace of blessing and thanksgiving we make for it. Praise God!   Amen.

56

As this food will nourish us, O Lord, may we also be a source of life and a gift to each other.   Amen.

57

Good morning, Lord! We offer You all we do, think, and say today beginning with this breakfast.   Amen.

58

Bless this food to our service, dear Lord, and us to Thy service.   Amen.
(Sister Maria Rose, I.H.M.)

59

May this bread be shared in true family fellowship, that at this table and beyond it, we can be signs of Your presence in our world. Amen.

(Sister Maria Rose, I.H.M.)

60

Let love be the sweetness and wisdom the seasoning at this table, O heavenly Father. Amen.

61

With all this good food before us, O Father, we are the guests at Your table, for everything belongs to You.   Amen.

62

Dear Lord, grant that we might be truly grateful for the food set before us, which so many others less fortunate than we must do without.   Amen.

63

Food You give, if blest by You,
Will indeed our strength renew.
Grant it, Lord, we pray.   Amen.
(Sister M. Adelaide, O.P.)

64

At our table, Lord, preside,
As You food and drink provide.
      Be our honored Guest,
      This is our request.   Amen.
          (Sister M. Adelaide, O.P.)

65

      You, dear Lord, who brought conversion to Zacheus when You dined in his house, preside at our table conversation so that it may inspire us to renewed apostolic zeal and vigor.   Amen.
          (Sister M. Adelaide, O.P.)

66

God of goodness, bless our food.
Keep us in a pleasant mood.
Bless the cook and all who serve us.
From indigestion, Lord, preserve us.   Amen.
        (Abbey Press placemat #30103)

67

Forgive the cook and food, O Lord, and bless it
      all the same.

We hope You'll eat and drink with us and not regret You came.   Amen.
(Abbey Press placemat #30105)

68

Let us celebrate the fruit of God's goodness at this our meal.   Amen.
(Abbey Press placemat #30111)

69

Jesus, at the seashore You had ready for Your Apostles a charcoal fire with fish cooking on it; the Gospel adds there was bread. I like to think that in Your loving compassion You made toast for those hungry men (Jn. 21:9).   Thank You, Lord.
(Sister Joseph Clare, O.P.)

70

Let us taste some joy and happiness in this (dinner, supper) and in all the other blessings of God.   Amen.

71

Day is done. May we relax at this meal and rejoice each other in God.　Amen.

72

Take and eat and appreciate all the things the Lord has provided for at this table. Amen.

73

God is good. God is great. May He bless the food which we partake through Christ our Lord.　Amen.

(Sister Elena, O.P.)

74

If we eat of this food of earth, O Lord, grant that we likewise partake of the Bread of Your altar.　Amen.

75

Better this ordinary meal with Your love, Lord, than abundance without You. Amen.

76

May all flesh that is nourished by the food which You provide, heavenly Father, bless Your holy name forever. Through Christ our Lord. Amen.

(Sister Elena, O.P.)

77

Some have meat but cannot eat.
And some would eat but lack it.
But we have meat and we can eat,
And so the Lord be thanked.

(Robert Burns)

78

May we respect much more, O Lord, those with whom we eat than what we eat. Amen.

79

Let any quarrel end, dear Lord, as we spread this table before us.   Amen.

80

O God, from whom we receive all things, we praise You for Your gifts. It is through love You feed us, so bless also what You give. Amen.

(Translation from German)

81

Please God, let us "feed" each other as we eat together.   Amen.

82

May we eat in such a way, dear Lord, that our virtues are increased in Your sight. Amen.

83

Please safeguard, O Lord, both the necessity of eating and the pleasures of this table.   Amen.

O God, I pray I'll grateful be
For Your kindness and fidelity.
> Before me, now, Your gifts You place—
> Your food, Your drink, Your loving grace.
> Amen.
>> (Sister Regina Marie, O.P.)

Not like Adam and Eve who ate forbidden fruit may we eat at this table, Lord, but like Yourself who ate and drank at table in peace and contentment with Your apostles. Amen.

O Lord, we need Your help so that we use discretion and moderation in the necessity of eating and of food. Sustain us, dear Lord. Amen.

Dear God,
> For loving friends surrounding us,

we thank You.
Be with us in our feasting and rejoicing.
Amen.

(Sr. Regina Marie, O.P.)

88

May the salt on this table remind us of
the wisdom of our baptism, O Father; the bread,
of the altar; and the meat, of Thy incarnate
Word.   Amen.

89

In Thy providence, O God, we are here
at this table today. Keep us, we pray, always
under Your care. Through Christ our Lord.
Amen.

90

May our desire for food, O Father, be
not too costly or too dainty nor too hastily and
greedily eaten.   Amen.

Make us grateful, Lord, we pray;
Make us generous every day.
Bless us as we gather here.
Keep us in Your friendship, near.   Amen.
(Sr. Regina Marie, O.P.)

92

May our minds be made keener rather than dulled by the amount of food we eat, O Lord.   Amen.

93

Our mouths water before all this beautiful food. Thank You, Lord, for the joy of taste. Amen.

94

Let us place ourselves in God's presence.

Christ, we thank You for these our (brothers, sisters . . .); we are grateful for our (work, vocation . . .). In this spirit we partake of the food You have given us and we ask Your blessing.   Amen.

95

Let not our eating and drinking, O Lord, lead to levity or talkativeness, but rather to a balanced confidence and joy.   Amen.

96

May our longing for this food, dear Lord, remind us of our hunger for Your knowledge and love.   Amen.

97

Heavenly Father, we offer ourselves with this food to You, that as the meal nourishes us, so may we help each other to good. Amen.

98

Let not excessive eating and drinking at this celebration, O Lord, hinder in any way

our light of reason in following Your will.
Amen.

99

How precious, God is Your constant love!
    Men find protection under the shadow of
        Your wings.
They feast on the abundant food from
        Your house;
    You give them to drink from the river of
        Your goodness.
You are the source of all life.
    and because of Your light we see the light.
    Amen.

(Psalm 36)

100

May this wine drunken moderately with
this meal be a joy of our souls and cheer to our
hearts.　Amen.

(Eccles. 31:36)

101

As Your word descended at creation to
make new things for us, Lord, may it also de-

scend upon our food now to make it health-giving and good for us.   Amen.

102

Lord, it isn't easy to feed the world.
I would rather say my prayers regularly,
    properly;
I would rather abstain on Fridays,
I would rather visit my pauper,
I would rather give to fairs and orphanages;
But apparently that isn't enough.
It's nothing, if one day You can say to me:
    "I was hungry."

(Michel Quoist)

103

O Lord, refresh our sensibilities. Give us this day our daily taste. Restore to us soups that spoons will not sink in, and sauces which are never the same twice. Raise up among us stews with more gravy than we have bread to blot it with, and casseroles that put starch and substance in our limp modernity. Take away our fear of fat, and make us glad of the oil which ran upon Aaron's beard. Give us pasta with a hundred fillings, and rice in a thousand variations. Above all, give us grace to live as true men—to fast till we come to a refreshed sense of what we have and then to dine gratefully on all that comes to hand. Drive far from us, O Most Bountiful, all creatures of air and darkness; cast out the demons that possess us; deliver us from the fear of calories and the bondage of nutrition; and set us free once more in our own land, where we shall serve Thee as Thou hast blessed us—with the dew of heaven, the fatness of the earth, and plenty of corn and wine.   Amen.

(Rev. Robert Farrar Capon)

104

May Christ through this food add to our peace among us during this meal.   Amen.

105

A mother's (father's, etc.) care is in this food, O Lord. Bless each for the service to us Amen.

106

As Mary served at Cana, may we serve each other at this table, O Lord.   Amen.

107

Come, O Jesus, be our guest, and share with us what You have provided.   Amen.

(my mother's prayer)

108

With life ahead of us and with food before us, O Lord, may we relish both for You. Amen.

109

You are remembered most at a meal, dear Lord. Let our eating reflect the love of Your Supper.   Amen.

110

At table You forgave the sins of Magdalen, O Lord.

May our thanks to You now be our perfume in this room (house, etc.).   Amen.

111

Let us feast at this table, Lord, on graciousness as well as on food.   Amen.

112

Through Your Holy Spirit, O Father, may we come to see the blessedness of this food and meal together.

Through Christ our Lord.   Amen.

113

May God be praised for caring for us at this meal.   Amen.

114

Let us taste and see the goodness of the Lord at this meal.   Amen.

115

As often as we eat together, O Father, let us become more united to You.

Through Christ our Lord.   Amen.

116

Whether we eat or drink, let us do so moderately for the Lord.   Amen.

117

You delight us, Lord, in the good things
of taste. Thank You for providing this pleasure
for us.   Amen.

118

With the same mouths by which we eat
we praise Your goodness, O Lord.   Amen.

PRAYERS AFTER MEALS

1

Your blessings, O Lord, give us constant cause to say, "God is great!" (Ps. 40:26) We thank You for them all.   Amen.

2

We thank You for the abundance and variety of the foods You give us, Lord.   Amen.

3

Thank You, Father, for giving us bodily nourishment.

Please continue to supply all our spiritual needs too.   Amen.

4

Happiness is enjoying and sharing this meal, O Lord.

We thank You for making it possible. Amen.

5

Feast or fast. Either is a joyous response to Your goodness, O Lord. For one, we say, "Thank You, yes," and for the other we say, "Not now, thanks." But both are "Thank You," and that is what counts.   Amen.

6

Thank You, Lord, for this happy meal.

Please provide for many more like it. Amen.

7

Thank You, O holy Trinity, for the pleasures and provisions of this table today. Amen.

8

We thank You, O Lord, for Yourself and all the good things You allow to us—like this meal together.   Amen.

9

May we live generously and merrily as a result of this meal together.
Thank You for it all.   Amen.

10

Bless the Lord, you (fruits, etc.)
Bless the Lord, you (meats, etc.)
Bless us all who ate at this table(s).   Amen.

11

Thank You for the food we eat,
Thank You for the birds that sing
Thank You, God for everything.   Amen.
(Traditional)

12

We thank You, gracious Father, for the sun that developed our food, for the harvest of laborers that packaged it, and for our cook(s) who prepared this (breakfast, dinner, etc.) Amen.

13

To say our thanks to You now, dear Lord, is to make a "eucharist" of it, for that is what the word means.
We thank You.   Amen.

14

We give Thee thanks, O Lord, like Jesus at His Last Supper, for these and all Thy benefits.   Amen.

15

Thank You, Lord, for our meal, and bless all those we love who cannot be with us today.   Amen.

(Mrs. Margaret Firth)

16

Master, You had compassion on Jairus' daughter by raising her to life. Then You told her parents to give her something to eat (Lk. 8:50-56). We thank You Lord, for Your loving solicitude then as now.   Amen.

(Sister Joseph Clare, O.P.)

17

Merrily we have feasted at this table, Lord. Be praised and thanked for so much plenty.   Amen.

18

Thank You, thank You, Lord, for this beautiful table and for the loving company at this meal.   Amen.

19

May we sing praise to You day and night, O Lord, and always give thanks for your great care.   Amen.

Zacheus returned Your visit, dear Lord, with generous response to grace. We thank You for the inspiration we have received through Your presence at our table conversation. Amen.
(Sister M. Adelaide, O.P.)

21

As Your bounteous gifts we praise
Grateful hearts to You we raise.
Stay with us, dear Lord, we pray,
Through the labors of the day. Amen.
(Sister M. Adelaide, O.P.)

22

Now we with gratitude partake
Of food our work has won.
Dear Jesus, bless the humble meal
We eat when day is done. Amen.
(Sister M. Adelaide, O.P.)

23

Lord, we thank You for this food we have, and pray that soon all men have as much as we have to be thankful for. Amen.

24

We thank You, O Father, for the generosity of this meal, and we ask You to remember those departed who once took food with us in our home.   Amen.

25

For all our benefactors of this meal, we thank You, Lord.   Amen.

26

Thank You for the meal we've had. That we remember this blessing forever in our hearts we ask You, Lord, to help us.   Amen.

(Gerald Mohr)

27

We're grateful, Lord, for this food that we've worked for and prepared. We're grateful, Lord, for the food of the spirit that we could not earn but which You share so freely.   Amen.

(Sister Maria Rose, I.H.M.)

Maybe what we had for dinner tonight was not our favorite, but thanks, Lord, for letting something be there when we needed it, because we know there are very many that have nothing at all.   Amen.

We thank You, O Father, for the joy of having guests to share our meal.   Amen.

For the poor, dear Lord, we pray.
Satisfy their needs today.
As we thank You for this meal
Ease their hunger, we appeal.   Amen.
(Sister M. Adelaide, O.P.)

Lord, we thank You for Your care,
Food and drink, our daily fare.   Amen.
(Sister M. Adelaide, O.P.)

32

He makes us remember His wonders.
The Lord is compassion and love. He gives
food to those who fear Him. Glory to the Father,
and to the Son, and to the Holy Spirit.   Amen.
(Dominican Breviary)

33

Dear God,
Accept the thanks from hearts sincere,
For the food and drink You give us here.
Amen.

(Sr. Regina Marie, O.P.)

34

For food and drink and all good things
Praise and thanks to You our Lord.
You gave and will in future give
The food we need to live.   Amen.
(Translation from the German)

35

Thank You for a healthy appetite, Lord.
It is good to be here at this meal.   Amen.

36

Rub-a dub, dub,
Thanks for the grub,
Yea a a a h, Lord.   Amen.

(teenage prayer)

37

Thank You, Lord, for good health, abundant nutrition, fine digestion, and the togetherness at this table.   Amen.

38

You have originated these once-living
animals and plants as food for us, Lord. Thank
You for sharing Your creations with us.   Amen.

39

These may have been just leftovers,
Lord, but the food is still from Your garden.
Thank You.   Amen.

40

From all eternity, O Lord, out of love
for us, You planned this meal. Thank You.
(Sr. Regina Marie, O.P.)

41

We greet You, Christ;
We thank You, too
For all we have received from You.   Amen.
(Sr. Regina Marie, O.P.)

42

O Giver of gifts,
   May we never forget
To thank You for all
   That, before us, You set.   Amen.
(Sr. Regina Marie, O.P.)

43

The birds can sing;
The leaves can rustle;
The animals, frolic in glee;

44

But only we can thank You, Lord,
For Your loving fidelity.
Make us grateful.   Amen.

(Sr. Regina Marie, O.P.)

44

Dear God,
Let us seek You in peace and rejoicing;
Let us find You in sorrow and pain.
Let us thank You with joy when rejoicing;
Let us trust You, with love, to remain.
Amen.

(Sr. Regina Marie, O.P.)

FOR SPECIAL TIMES, PLACES AND PERSONS

SPECIAL OCCASIONS

On this beautiful feast (day, occasion) we offer You, O Lord, not only our hearts and souls but our very food and joys.   Amen.

For the companionship which has enhanced the joy of our festivity, we thank You, Lord. Grant that it may unite us more closely in the bonds of (sisterly, brotherly) love.   Amen.

(Sister Adelaide, O.P.)

Join us, Lord, in our joyful feast;
May our love and thanks, each day, increase.
Amen.

(Sister Regina Marie, O.P.)

46

Christ, today is a joyous feast. We thank You for it. We are grateful for the beautiful companionship of our fellow guests at this table. Please bless our food, bless all of us, and help us to spread Your joy.   Amen.

(Sister Frances Maureen, O.P.)

Every day is God's Day and today is a special day of (jubilee, marriage, etc.). Let us ask the blessing of God on our food, on each of us here, and on the poor of the world. In the name of the Father . . . etc.   Amen.

(Sister Frances Maureen, O.P.)

SPECIAL PERSONS

Dieters

Ah, Lord, help me to say "No" to myself before some of this food, but "Yes" always to Your will.   Amen.

Holy Family

O Lord, give us a true appreciation of the simplicity and beauty of Your meals in Nazareth. Make ours, too, a holy family.   Amen.

(Sister Regina Marie, O.P.)

Today as we sit down at this table let us remember the love of Mary as she prepared food for her Son.

O Christ, Son of Mary, bless our food as You blessed the daily bread taken with Mary and Joseph.   Amen.

(Sister Frances Maureen, O.P.)

Father's Day

Father of family: "Dear Lord, we thank You for all Your gifts. We thank You for (mention food on table.)" (Now each in turn mentions his own name . . . Mom thanks You. George thanks You, etc.)

Mary

Holy Mary, Mother of God, pray for us and all those we love now as we take our meal at this hour.   Amen.

Mother's Day

We eat this meal at our family gathering, O Lord, to celebrate our Mothers. Bless and protect them all, we pray.   Amen.

Nameday

With Saint N . . . we thank You, O gracious Father, for supplying all our needs of body and soul.   Amen.

Visitors

May our guests at this meal, O Father, share our friendships with each other.   Amen.

SPECIAL TIMES

Advent

Bless, Lord, Your gifts which of Your goodness we are about to receive; as we wait for the coming of Your Son, sustain us in mind and body: through Christ our Lord.   Amen.
(Liturgical Commission of Irish Dominican Province)

You have said, O Lord: "Wherever there are two or three gathered together in My name, there am I in the midst of them." We believe in Your word—Lord, come! Let us experience Your presence among us as we share this food in Your name.　Amen.

(Sister Marie de Lourdes, O.P.)

In gratitude to You today, O Lord, we say "Thank You" not only for the meal we have shared and enjoyed together but also for all Your gifts—the gifts of creation, Incarnation, redemption, and as well of individual talent, graces, and (religious, married, single) vocation. We say thank You, Lord.　Amen.

(Sister Marie de Lourdes, O.P.)

Ascension

May we as citizens of heaven and of earth share this meal in time so as to be more worthy of heaven.　Amen.

Christmas

Like the shepherds of Bethlehem, O Father, may we take this meal in simplicity of taste and in wonder at Your bounty. Through Christ our Lord.   Amen.

While we abound in plenty, Lord
This joyous Christmastide,
We ask Your blessing on the poor.
Please, Lord, their needs provide.   Amen.
(Sister Adelaide, O.P.)

Lord, we have joyfully received Your Son as our redeemer: may we receive this food, and all Your gifts as a pledge of the final gift of everlasting life with You.   Amen.
(Liturgical Commission of
Irish Dominican Province)

Dear Lord, here before us is spread our bountiful Christmas dinner. We ask You to bless all who helped to provide for it; those who planned it; those who prepared it and will serve it. Bless us also who are about to enjoy it. Amen.
(Sister Adelaide, O.P.)

This day, dear Son of God, You came to earth. You were Your Father's greatest gift to us. Make us grateful and generous with our gifts to others, as at this meal.   Amen.
(Sister Regina Marie, O.P.)

Sing to "O Tannenbaum"
O dinner bell, O dinner bell!
Thou bell most good and lovely!
The sound of thee at Christmastide
Spreads food and gladness far and wide.
O dinner bell, O dinner bell!
Thou hast a tasty message.

Bethlehem—House of Bread! Divine Infant, daily we are the recipients of Your gifts—in many forms. For all Your goodness we thank You. This our Christmas dinner is a symbol of our union with each other and with You. We ask Your blessing.   Amen.
(Sister Frances Maureen, O.P.)

Help us in our thanks
   to bend our strength
      day by day
   toward a Christmas
      yet to come:
   when all men
      of every stock and branch,
      of every color and nation,
         will sit down to table
         and join hands in peace.

This we ask
         through Your Son, our brother,
         who comes to us again

today and all days,
Christ Jesus the Lord.   Amen.
                    (Lawrence E. Moser, S.J.)

Our joyful hearts we lift in praise
And gratitude to You, dear Lord.
While "Merry Christmas, one and all"
Again we say with one accord.   Amen.
                    (Sister Adelaide, O.P.)

Easter

May we have on our wedding garment,
O Lord, at this feast of Your glorious resurrection.   Amen.

Bless, Lord, Your gifts and fill us with
Easter joy; may the food we are about to receive
from Your hand remind us of the first-fruits of
the new creation.   Amen.
                    (Liturgical Commission of
                    Irish Dominican Province)

Our Risen Lord bade you partake
Of food He spread at Galilee's lake.
Disciples, we would welcome you
To share this meal He blesses, too.   Amen.
                    (Sister Adelaide, O.P.)

To prove that You had risen, Lord,
You asked for food on Easter night.
Now we, on this bright Easter Day
Would serve You to our hearts' delight.
      Come, Lord, be our Easter Guest.   Amen.
           (Sister Adelaide, O.P.)

O Welcome Guest,
   Your love we know.
Remain with us;
   Your grace bestow.   Amen.
           (Sister Regina Marie, O.P.)

O You who rose in glory,
   You who conquered death and sin;
Break bread with us, this evening.
   Dear Guest divine, come in.   Amen.
           (Sister Regina Marie, O.P.)

With us, dear Lord, You shared today
Not bodily food alone.
Your Risen Body we received
To make us all Your own.
   For these we thank You, Lord.   Amen.
           (Sister Adelaide, O.P.)

Since the empty tomb,
nothing matters except everything—
   and everything is God's.
      And this food
         which we are about to receive

in the love of Your risen Son
is Your sign to us
    that nothing passes away,
    that nothing shall be lost,
    but that all shall be changed
    and touched with newness of life
            in Your Spirit.   Amen.
                    (Lawrence E. Moser, S.J.)

At Your resurrection, Lord, all nature arises in the new awakening of spring. The very bread before us has risen by the yeast in it. Thank You for surrounding us with the images of Your victory.   Amen.

Dear Risen Lord, we give You thanks
For faith renewed by Your kind deed.
Our hearts imbue with trust anew
As You supply our every need.   Amen.
                    (Sister Adelaide, O.P.)

Holy Thursday
May we be present to each other at this supper, dear Lord, as You were in the midst of Your Apostles.   Amen.

Lent

Bless, Lord, Your gifts which of Your goodness we are about to receive; may our observance of Lent cleanse us from sin, and make us hunger and thirst after justice. Amen.

(Liturgical Commission of
Irish Dominican Province)

O Lord, I like a full plate, but help me not to take second portions of the food I like on this table.   Amen.

Party

Thanks, Lord, for the food, drink, and fun we have shared at this table.   Amen.

Picnic

Food of hot.
Food of cold.
Bless this, Lord,
Before it molds.   Amen.

(James Murnan)

Patriotic
July 4

Dear God,
You made us free. Keep us free to love

You. Make us mindful of Your providential care. Through Christ our Lord.   Amen.

(Sister Regina Marie, O.P.)

Our Father,
    You have given us this food,
                this home,
                one another,
        only that we may decide
            either to share in the creation of love
                and unity,
            or destroy and pass our days in fear.

We thank You, Father, for the good things of
    this world,
            and for the power of choice,
for this is the glory of Your own life.
We ask that we may be worthy of it
        in Christ Jesus,
            Your Son and our Brother.   Amen.

(Lawrence E. Moser, S.J.)

Pentecost

    As we relish this food, let us be moved by Thy Spirit to experience You, our God. Through Christ our Lord.   Amen.

Through Your Spirit may we get to know You, O God, by this simple gathering at our table.   Amen.

Come into our souls anew, O Holy Spirit, far more intimately than this food about to enter our bodies. Through Christ our Lord. Amen.

We pray You, Lord, that Your Holy Spirit may enlighten our minds; and as we partake of this food, may our bodies be strengthened so that we may daily serve You more faithfully.   Amen.

(Liturgical Commission of
Irish Dominican Province)

Holy Spirit—Spirit of peace, of joy, of love—be with us and fill our hearts to over-flowing. Bless our food and grant that as we eat it, we may be aware of our hungry fellow-men with a concern that becomes action. In the name of the Father . . . etc.

(Sister Frances Maureen, O.P.)

Thanksgiving

Let's thank God for what we have to eat
On this gay and festive feast.

Although we have much more than others
We must remember they are all our brothers.
   Amen.

(Thomas Gregg)

"Thank You, thank You",
      We gratefully pray,
For the food and drink
      You give us this day.   Amen.

(Sister Regina Marie, O.P.)

Never a day goes by, dear God,
      Without Your tender care.
Teach us to think of others, too:
      Help us, with joy, to share.   Amen.

(Sister Regina Marie, O.P.)

Keep us thankful,
Father,
so that we may touch all things,
   and all men
      only with the delicacy
      of reverence and love.
Keep us aware of the work
Your work,
that You have given into our hands.
For only in Your Spirit
      will Your kingdom come,
      and that day shine

when ALL men will see clearly
that there is indeed reason
for thanksgiving.   Amen.
(Lawrence E. Moser, S.J.)

May this meal with each other express
the joy and gladness of this happy day (Christmas, Easter, Thanksgiving, etc.).   Amen.

Trinity

God the Father, sanctify us; God the
Son, bless our food; God, the Holy Spirit, fill
us with Your peace and joy.   Amen.
(Sister Frances Maureen, O.P.)

GENERAL ANY DAY PRAYERS

Dear God,
We bow our heads,
And humbly pray,
"Bless food and drink
And US today."   Amen.
(Sister Regina Marie, O.P.)

In Your presence, O God, we eat our
humble meal today. Through Christ our Lord.
Amen.